Stephen Donald Huff's

PROMPT-GENERATED MEDIA USING ARTIFICIAL INTELLIGENCE

An Author's Guide

CAPITAL IDEATIONS LLC

Published by Capital Ideations LLC
2733 Palermo Ct.
League City, TX 77573

© Wednesday, January 8, 2025
Printed in the United States of America
Copyright © Stephen Donald Huff, 2025
First published in the United States of America by Capital
Ideations LLC, 2025

ISBN-13: 979-8306382739

Readers Rave About Stephen Donald Huff!

Must buy! (Terminus I - III [Conquest]: A Terminus Series Compendium)
"It was a great read! So good, I read it twice!"
--*Rebecca (May 25, 2019)*

A Helluva Lot of Fun! (Terminus)
"Terminus kept me guessing and thinking the entire time. It is not what I expected but, in the end, I really ended up enjoying it a LOT... worth noting is this is a post-apocalyptic book... Keep your mind open and prepare to be entertained."
--*Gregory D. Wehn (September 19, 2016)*

Strong Male Character and Strong Female Character Surviving Hell Because to Survive Means That Others Will Die! (Terminus)
"Terminus is a strange interesting story about the apocalypse. There a lot of twists and turns that will lead to area 51. I highly recommend this book and intend to read other books by this author. "
--*Modupe Hendricks (April 9, 2016)*

This Turned Out to Be a Surprisingly Fun Read! Chock Full of New Ideas! (Terminus)
"This turned out to be a surprisingly fun read chock full of new ideas. The world building is intriguing (mankind has been decimated by a signal that disinhibits our darkest tendencies) and the main characters are clearly complicated and - to some extent - less susceptible to this influence than are many others. I really enjoyed it. Nicely done!"
--*Tensai (September 11, 2016)*

Great (Terminus)
"A good story all round. Plot, action, originality, characters, and flow all get a big fat tick. How apocalyptic sci fi horror should be done."
--*Bean Bag (43176)*

Five Stars! (The Serpentine)
"Truly good read"
--*Steven Burget (April 22, 2016)*

A Twisty, Warp-Jumping Ride Through Space That Is Hellishly Fun! (The Serpentine)
"Huff's take on a fairly well-known genre is unique and fresh. I highly recommend this to fans of sci-fi and general probing into the human psyche when under duress. As I put it down it made me think about how one may react and survive in similar circumstances faced by the characters and reflect back upon how these situations still apply to life as it is now."
--*Gregory D. Wehn (November 14, 2016)*

Continues to Purl Amazing Storylines Time and Time Again! (Dark Matter)
"Some writers (another Stephen comes to mind) have an endless well of creativity and ideas for story after story after story. This reader doesn't know how this Stephen, Stephen Donald Huff, continues to purl amazing storylines time and time again. Since this writer is sure to not disappoint, one can only encourage such prolific bounty for many stories to come. Thank you, for showing us how it is done with such grace and ease!"
--*Amazon Customer (June 1, 2016)*

A Great Collection of Adult Stories! (Death Eidolons)
"Stephen Huff's writing is vivid and his stories are rich in conflict. The stories have a disturbing quality that sustained my interest from one to another. They leave a sort of "Outer Limits" impression. I hope to read more of his work. This book provided hours of reading enjoyment."
--*DataJanitor (June 9, 2016)*

Dark and Gritty Shorts! Good Reading! (Wee, Wicked Whispers)
"For those who like your comedy tragic and dark. Huff's writing is clever, intriguing, intense and every now and again gruesome. These Twilight Zonesque stories pick away at your mind. They are well written, often brutal, sometimes gory but a collection worth reading."
--*Allison Leinbach (June 8, 2013)*

Fiction Novels and Novellas

Havoc
Slate Gardens
A Cult of Fat Stanley (Novella)
Live-Jack (Novella)

A Tapestry of Twisted Threads in Folio

Of Heroes, None
Of Victors, Few
Of Losers, Legions
Of Conspirators, Four
Of Deviants, Five
Of Soldiers, Six
Of Monsters, Seven
Of Pranksters, Eight
Of Lovers, Nine
Of Plagues, Ten
Of Aliens, Eleven
Of Mysteries, Twelve
Of Rogues, Thirteen
Of Afflictions, Fourteen
Of Phantoms, Flights

Short Story Collections

Shores of Silver Seas
Wee, Wicked Whispers
Violence Redeeming
Death Eidolons
Dark Matter
Nightland

For your dreams; I hope this guide brings them a step closer.

TABLE OF CONTENTS

INTRODUCTION

Introduction

This Author's Guide will aid the novice reader's attempt to rapidly and effectively use Artificial Intelligence (AI) to generate quality media via textual prompts. Targeted media includes image-, video-, voice-, and music-formatted outputs, as well as any AI product generated via prompt.

This Author's Guide presents an essential, formalized method for creating well-considered and meaningfully structured text that will rationally translate into media output in a systematic and reliably iterative fashion. While each generative AI model (*e.g.*, Aitubo *versus* MS Designer) may present a variety of configurations to manage subtle variations of output, a properly formalized prompt should produce reliably consistent results from one format and from one system to the next.

Instructionals and illustrations included within this guide are succinct and minimalized to trim the reader's learning experience and expedite the thought-to-publication process. Since these methodologies are all very new the author will update this text often; as such, the reader should periodically revisit and reload this document to review its latest insights.

NOTE: at the time of this writing, this guide relies upon Aitubo for all media output. Any similar prompt-driven system will benefit from the methods described below.

Introduction

RULES FOR EFFECTIVE PROMPTS

The following general rules of composition will guide the reader at a glance. These entries will change over time as this Author's Guide and the underlying technology evolve.

- Simplicity is clarity.
- Verify spelling, grammar, and composition.
- Describe/label the bare minimum.
- Match format to output.
- Explore with the generic format.
- Let the AI guide, then adapt.
- Give durable components unique labels.
- Tradeoff between the explicit and implicit.
- Use control symbols appropriately.
- Use present tense for action.

Simplicity is clarity. Use small, meaningful words. A more descriptive prompt may be less reproduceable than a simpler prompt. When describing a concept, research the proper terminology – sometimes the proper term improves clarity of the output (unfortunately, when the concept is specialized, a more generic term may serve better). Experiment.

Verify spelling, grammar, and composition. Hallucinations (unwanted, surreal artefacts) are often the result of typographical, syntactical or semantical errors. For example, if the output should include a single hand, an incidental secondary use of the plural, 'hands', may cause additional appendages to randomly appear within the output.

Describe/label the bare minimum. Hallucinations (unwanted, surreal artefacts) may also result from extraneous input. For example, if the output should include only a closeup 'headshot', do not include a description of shoes or socks or other objects that might direct perspective away from the desired focus. Otherwise, these unnecessarily included components may appear in an undesirable way.

Match format to output. Production of media will somewhat rely upon the compositional space provided. For example, if a panorama landscape is desired in a graphical output, a vertical format may unnecessarily constrain and challenge the AI agent – for this output, a horizontal format may support superior results.

Explore with the generic format. AI agents are capable of great things, yet they are also likely to be constrained after one fashion or another. These agents will not produce output that was not presented to the underlying models during training. Requesting complex or explicit output may produce problematic renditions. Explore possibilities with the generic format (*e.g.*, the square format for 2D images), then observe capabilities and adapt to training-based bias and format-oriented constraints.

Let the AI guide, then adapt. Complex compositions may challenge the AI agent. Exploratory prompts should begin one of two ways: 1) simply, or 2) elaborately. When simplicity fails, the second style may actually provide benefit. Provide a verbose prompt, observe AI capabilities, and then adapt the prompt accordingly. For example, if the AI agent consistently depicts a silver bracelet on a character's wrist, either add the bracelet to the generative prompt, or explicitly describe the character's wrist as being bare.

Give durable components unique labels. Avoid confusing the generative AI agent. Do this by providing unique, standout names and labels for durable characters and components. For example, to create a durable character that depicts a specific 'cow', do not label the component 'COW'; rather, a more unique (non-word) label may produce superior results. For example, use 'ACOW' or 'THECOW' or 'WHITECOW', etc..., to label and differentiate a durable cow-character (by individualized name) from every other cow in the composition.

Tradeoff between the explicit and implicit. Implicit prompts may produce fabulous and otherwise un-directable content into the output, since implicit directions provide 'wiggle-room' for the AI to 'hallucinate' (produce random and sometimes surreal artefacts in the composition). When this adds to the quality of output, use it. When the opposite result ensues, provide a more explicit prompt.

Use control symbols appropriately. Prompt-driven AI systems typically train on the same kind of input that the reader will provide – that is, text. Human beings use control symbols (punctuation) to clarify and organize meaning within textual compositions, and so AI agents will do the same after training on this kind of input. Use of periods, semi-colons and colons may provide helpful clues that can dramatically improve the orientation and organization of output.

Use present tense for action. Action can be difficult to produce via prompt-driven AI generation. Use of present tense implies action that helpfully clues the AI agent to depict objects in motion. For example, 'a cat is preening' may produce better results than 'a preening cat'. Also, direction of action, that is the indication of this-action happening to that-thing, is often most difficult to achieve;

at this time, best practice uses a mixture of language and positional placement within the prompt to achieve desired outcomes. Most of the time.

SETTING THE SCENE

Setting the Scene

For illustrative purposes, this guide begins with the production of simple two-dimensional graphics via essential text-based descriptions. The techniques presented within this Author's Guide will serve equally well with any media format (video, music, etc...). In this case, a simple prompt generates a series of scenes that may be useful as backgrounds – or as a starting point for the broader instructional that follows.

Begin with a generic (and not very useful) series of prompts and their (square, 2D) output:

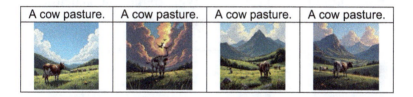

| A cow pasture. | A cow pasture. | A cow pasture. | A cow pasture. |

These images result from the same system and identical prompt. Notice the variation.

Sometimes, this randomized output is desired. Most often, however, the reader will require a more controlled output.

Composition of output may benefit from scene-setting (SS). Scene and setting typically rely upon a description of the who, what, where, when, how (if not the why) of a thing.

Graphic-comic realism; morning. A cow pasture.	Graphic-comic realism; morning. A cow pasture.	Graphic-comic realism; morning. A cow pasture.	Graphic-comic realism; morning. A cow pasture.

Here, the prompt specifies a compositional style (*'...graphic-comic realism...'*) and time of day (*'...morning...'*). Results are more consistent, but again notice the variation.

The first part of the SS statement describes the quality or style of desired rendition. In the above results, output presents an illustrative style. In the results below, the prompt produces a more realistic image.

Photographic realism; morning. A cow pasture.	Photographic realism; morning. A cow pasture.	Photographic realism; morning. A cow pasture.	Photographic realism; morning. A cow pasture.

Here, the prompt specifies a photo-realistic compositional style (*'...photographic realism...'*) and time of day (*'...morning...'*). Overall composition is consistent with the previous results, only the quality of output has changed to reflect this scene-setting input.

For both sets of results, notice the focus on a single cow. Why? Perhaps because this prompt specifies a (*'...a cow pasture...'*) rather than 'a pasture full of cows'.

Graphic-comic realism; morning. A pasture full of cows.	Graphic-comic realism; morning. A pasture full of cows.	Graphic-comic realism; morning. A pasture full of cows.	Graphic-comic realism; morning. A pasture full of cows.

Again, focus tends toward a single cow, but now the output includes a more prominent herd of cows in the background. Perhaps the focus is constrained by output format. Where the prompt should produce a panorama, for example, a horizontal format might provide benefit.

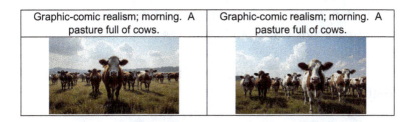

Graphic-comic realism; morning. A pasture full of cows.	Graphic-comic realism; morning. A pasture full of cows.

In the above set of results, a wider output format brings the background objects closer to the viewer. Emphasis also improves.

Notice the coming and going of the sun. Perhaps this occurs because the prompt generically described the time of day. The next prompt-result set provides an essential (and the suggested) format for description of scene and setting.

Graphic-comic realism; sunrise, sky is colored purple, crimson, and gold, Austin, Texas, 2025AD, 9AM.

A pasture full of cows.

The above result provides the essential and suggested form of a scene-setting statement. In addition to the text, notice the added spatial structure – this use of whitespace aids clarity and improves the prompt's reusability.

Suggested components of the SS statement include (but are not restricted to):

- Output style (*e.g.*, graphic-comic realism).
- Special considerations (*e.g.*, this prompt specifies 'sunrise' to ensure the sun is visible).
- Compositional palette (*e.g.*, this prompt provides colors to ensure the sky is depicted consistently). NOTE: providing a descriptive term like 'sunrise' within an interior scene will probably depict the sun through a window (for example); when this result is not required, simply rely on the next section of the SS to specify daylight (or moonlight).
- Location, date and time; while not always required to such a specific level of expression, generic placement of a

composition provides clues to the AI agent
that will aid its provision of extraneous
detail (or lack thereof). It is this extraneous
detail that can either make AI output vibrant
and believable or, alternatively, provide
frustrating points of variation that prohibit
consistent depictions of durable characters
or things.

In principle, the SS should be one-line, simple, and
concise. The SS should lead the prompt and stand alone at
the top of each input, both to clue the AI agent and to
provide a visual frame of reference to the reader as prompt
complexity increases.

Use of a proper scene-setting statement is not
always required. Indeed, sometimes it is not helpful. Most
often, however, epic compositions will benefit from
consistent, explicit management of scene and setting.

Setting the Scene

PRECEDENCE, ORDER, AND PLACEMENT

Setting the Scene

After scene and setting, one of the more difficult aspects of directing AI generated output via textual prompt will likely be the precedence, order, and placement (POP) of key (explicit) elements within the composition. Most often, POP within the output will depend upon POP within the prompt.

Graphic-comic realism; sunrise, sky is colored purple, crimson, and gold, Austin, Texas, 2025AD, 9AM.

Foreground: a sunflower.

Background: a pasture full of cows.

Here, the prompt places certain objects into the foreground and background of the output. Within such a simple scene this might seem unnecessary – and it probably is within this specific example. Improved direction within the prompt will most often (but not always) translate into improved consistency within the product. Without this kind of control, the AI agent will make its own 'decisions' about the order of such things, and variation will ensue.

What happens when the prompt reverses these explicit directions, 'foreground' and 'background'?

Graphic-comic realism; sunrise, sky is colored purple, crimson, and gold, Austin, Texas, 2025AD, 9AM.

Background: a pasture full of cows.

Foreground: a sunflower.

The above results correspond very well to the initial results. Clearly, spatial orientation of these statements within the prompt fails to significantly alter the outcome. The reason may seem obvious, but the truth is not so direct.

Unlike 'rule-driven' software systems, the terms 'foreground' and 'background' are not explicitly encoded within AI systems as control words. Instead, training data influences these outcomes in a much more nuanced way simply because most people use these terms when describing graphic media. As with young students learning to read, the AI 'artist' will naturally take clues and cues from terms that appear frequently during training.

The informed reader will take advantage of this phenomenon to improve the quality of prompt-generated products. Incidentally, this is true for many other aspects of generative AI performance. During refinement of prompt and output, the informed reader will draw intuition from this circumstance to rapidly produce meaningful, productive text-based directives. As with the next example.

Graphic-comic realism; sunrise, sky is colored purple, crimson, and gold, Austin, Texas, 2025AD, 9AM.

Background: a pasture full of cows.

Foreground: a sunflower.

A short clown. An obese dog. A furry cat.

The above prompt provides three new components at the end of the statement, outside its framing of foreground and background (which are still reversed in order). Notice the absence of the clown and dog, which have been hallucinated into a single clown-dog object. This result may be interesting, but it is probably not generally desirable.

Most likely, this hallucination stems from the obvious confusion of organization within the prompt, as well as a lack of action within the scene. Here, the word 'action' means use of present tense verbs (*e.g.*, 'a cat is preening' rather than 'a preening cat', which uses the gerund). More on this later.

Sometimes POP statements will be clearly that – a statement of precedence, order, or placement. Other times POP becomes an expression of technical skill or of artistic talent. Intuition helps. So, what is POP?

Precedence comes first because it is the most ephemeral aspect of the overall POP concept. As such, it is perhaps its most important detail.

Within the context of this Author's Guide, 'precedence' refers to the total compositional order of the required outcome. At its simplest, a precedence statement is a word or brief phrase that establishes this concept in both the prompt and the output. Conceptually, utilization of precedence is a bit more complex.

Within the above example, this concept is most apparent within the prompt's overall layout. Organization of components, phrases, punctuation and words all provide clues of precedence.

The suggested prompt-component order is 1) scene-setting statement, 2) foreground statement, 3) background statement, and, finally, 3) durable character/object descriptions. In addition to this essential order (separated by whitespace for readability) the above example provides two explicit clues by defining both *'Foreground:'* and *'Background:'* elements. Most of the time, this is enough.

Ultimately, from here the concept becomes considerably more nuanced. At times, moving the background statement to the very end of the prompt – that is after character descriptions – or shifting a crucial character/component description forward above all other elements might clue the AI agent to produce variant output. Finally, experiment with phrase order, word order, and punctuation to manipulate emphasis or grouping.

In the middle because the concept presents two equally useful meanings, order-statements describe the order of things. No mystery there. Yet expression of order may be apparent at both a microscopic and macroscopic scale within the prompt. What does this mean?

Most of the time, placing one component before another within the text is enough, as with '...*OBJ1 is tumbling; OBJ2 is shattering; OBJ3 is...*'. When this produces an unsatisfactory result, be more explicit with the prompt language, perhaps provide '...*OBJ1 is tumbling in front of OBJ2; OBJ2 is shattering in front of OBJ3; OBJ3 is...*'.

Again, more subtly, order is also just that – order. Most AI agents will place OBJ1 before OBJ2 given the prompt above, while '...*OBJ2 is shattering; OBJ1 is tumbling; OBJ3 is...*' will most often present OBJ2 in the foreground.

Beware! The naming or labelling of a durable component with a serial numeric like those presented above (bad author!) may have strange effects – this is because the numeric entries imply a precedence of their own. These AI agents are mathematical creatures, after all. The reader may benefit from giving durable characters and components names and labels that avoid the use of numerals. In this case, OBJA, OBJB, and OBJC might serve better.

Finally within the POP triad, placement statements are clear, simple textual clues that inform the AI agent regarding placement of key components within the output. The concept of placement also relates to the explicit order of a prompt's components.

For example, to avoid random placement of AGIRL within a scene, the reader might specify within the '*Foreground:*' statement '...*AGIRL is standing to the left of ANOBJ...*'. Of course, without additional detail regarding the placement of ANOBJ, the AGIRL character might depicted partially out of frame (since the prompt implicitly focuses ANOBJ as its center). A following phrase placing

ANOBJ in a specific location within the output frame would resolve this ambiguity.

As before, the difference between order and placement can be subtle. These concepts certainly overlap. For this reason, think of placement primarily as a phrase-level application of both precedence and order. For example, in a durable character description, two considerations become important.

First, placing descriptors that change often at the end of the description text-block will aid the reader's need to repeatedly cut or paste these data into place. This can be useful when characters are moving through various conditions that require alternating closeup and wide-angle views. By leaving a description of shoes at the end, for example, removal and addition of this attire enhances requests for associated framing statements – wide-angle with the shoes, closeup without them. Place the attire at the end for this requirement. Alternate needs can also be readily accommodated in this way (*e.g.*, a character might be physically 'morphing' into different shapes such that the most common edit target might be something other than attire.

Too, placement should refer to the macro-level organization of a composition. Move a durable character's action from the foreground to the background to emphasize one over another.

Consider this prompt:

```
Graphic-comic realism;
sunrise; Austin, Texas,
2025 AD, 9AM.

Foreground: CHARA is
dancing; CHARB is skulking
behind CHARA.

Background: a country
square dance.

CHARA is a female.

CHARB is a male.
```

Versus this prompt:

```
Graphic-comic realism;
sunrise; Austin, Texas,
2025 AD, 9AM.

Foreground: CHARA is
dancing.

Background: CHARB is
skulking; a country square
dance.

CHARA is a female.

CHARB is a male.
```

As regards the concept of placement, its most obvious meaning is clearly visible. Both within each prompt individually, and between both prompts, too.

Within the first, placement is explicit only – '...*CHARB is skulking behind CHARA...*'. This is a valid effort and will likely produce viable results. When this approach fails, something like the second prompt might represent a reasonable next attempt.

In the second, placement is also readily visible. CHARA is performing action explicitly within the foreground, while CHARB's action is occurring within the background definition. More subtly, CHARB's action is placed before the final background descriptor – this might serve to clue the AI agent as regards CHARB's placement within the overall composition, perhaps preventing it from being relegated to the background. Placement within a placement statement!

Subtility within subtility. This is the way people describe things. This is the way the AI agent trained. Fortunately, coming full circle, this is also the way you might describe things to exploit these phenomena.

Again, beware. Use of POP can act as a 'double edged sword'. Use it consistently within a prompt to explicitly manage a durable, reproduceable scene, or avoid it altogether to produce a more free-form (and less reproduceable) outcome.

Graphic-comic realism; sunrise, sky is colored purple, crimson, and gold, Austin, Texas, 2025AD, 9AM.

Foreground: a short clown is dancing; an obese dog is barking; a furry cat is preening.

Background: a pasture full of cows.

Within the output depicted above, in the foreground a clown is dancing, a cat is preening (sort of), and we see an obese dog. Moving these components to the background aspect of the prompt's POP would reduce the prominence of these components to that of the other background objects.

Incidentally, a note about the word 'preening'. Common verbs that are also common gerunds appear to confuse many AI agents at this time. For obvious reasons, since these concepts confuse many human beings, too.

This is likely why the cat's actions are less pronounced, more understated. In fact, it appears to simply sit there most of the time. The AI agent knew to draw a cat, but it appears to have abandoned any attempt to develop the action further. Improve this result by changing verbs and adding objectives, perhaps something like '...*a cat is bowing and licking its left paw...*'.

Indeed, notice the use of present tense action verbs throughout. This prompt provides '...*a clown is dancing...*' rather than '...*a dancing clown...*'. Here the verb-gerund tradeoff is less problematic for the AI agent, because the outcomes clearly present a clown, dancing.

Individual POP concepts – precedence, order and placement – may occasionally overlap, or not, yet do not suffer confusion. This Author's Guide is not a treatise on dogma. These are concepts and ideas intended to organize the reader's productions, true, yet more vitally these terms combine with all the lessons presented herein to comprise and present a simple message, which concludes this section.

Increasingly complex output will benefit from a more complex prompt, which will require some form of POP management. Prompts that fail to specify POP will produce results that tend to be more explicitly directed by the AI agent. Additional control within the prompt will typically provide more controlled output.

DURABLE CHARACTERS AND COMPONENTS

Durable Characters and Components

Production of individual 'one-off' compositions via prompt-driven AI generation does not require any special consideration as regards preservation of the output's contents and qualities. Yet more often the reader will benefit from the ability to reproduce objects intended to persist from one set of outputs to the next.

Application of a proper and formalized methodology for describing, maintaining and reusing characters and components will easily achieve this result. Without such a system, production of consistently durable objects can be frustratingly difficult.

Primarily, this result derives from effective naming/labelling of these resources. In addition to provisioning durable objects, use of a proper naming/labelling protocol visually organizes the prompt while providing a facile means for later referencing complex objects within the output. These conventions also facilitate copy-and-paste operations, such that a well-organized reader will quickly begin manipulating concrete 'things' rather than abstract text blocks within their prompts.

Graphic-comic realism; sunrise, sky is colored purple, crimson, and gold, Austin, Texas, 2025AD, 9AM.

Foreground: wide-angle view of ACHARACTER holding ANOBJECT.

Background: a pasture full of cows.

ACHARACTER is a clown.

ANOBJECT is a hardcover book.

That is one creepy clown! Here, the output accurately reflects the intentions of the prompt, even after abstraction via application of names and labels. Notice the use of ALLCAPS: this technique provides visual clues within increasingly complex inputs (and will eventually segue into a method for collecting individual prompts into a more epic composition, *e.g.* a video screenplay).

Also, notice the naming/labelling convention. While any name/label might serve, the reader must be careful not to use an actual word for these purposes; for example, the prompt might label the clown 'ROBERT' or 'JOAN' or whatever, but it should not label the clown as 'CLOWN' since other clowns might be required within the content.

Of course, without seed control (provision of a given number to start the AI system's random number generator, if any), each run of this prompt would potentially produce a different clown, since there are many styles of clown attire and makeup (as well as styles of persons playing the clown).

Expanding on the concept of naming/labelling, a prompt can easily reuse these components in a consistently durable way by providing a rather rigorous description of the character/object that is amenable to copy/paste operations. Easily achieve this effect by applying the basic rules previously described. Experiment with the underlying AI agent's preferences (since each agent likely trained on different inputs), and then adapt NL descriptors accordingly.

Graphic-comic realism; sunrise, sky is colored purple, crimson, and gold, Austin, Texas, 2025AD, 9AM.

Foreground: wide-angle view of ACHAR; ACHAR is holding ANOBJ; ANOBJ is open in the middle.

Background: a pasture full of cows.

ACHAR is a female clown with slender features; ACHAR is wearing a plain unadorned red jumpsuit with white ruffle cuffs and big round yellow buttons, a plain unadorned two-point jester's cap with golden balls dangling, white gloves, and black shoes; ACHAR has a white face, round red lips, a spherical red nose, black diamond eyes, and bright orange hair; ACHAR is 33 years old; ACHAR is 5'10" tall.

ANOBJ is a hardcover book with a plain unadorned red cover; ANOBJ has 100 pages.

The results above derive from the same prompt without seed (without an explicitly reproduceable starting point), yet each image is fairly consistent with the others. Still, variation persists.

In this outcome, for example, the reader can easily see the AI agent's preferences for depicting this kind of object (a clown). Note the waistline of the jumpsuit and the collars.

From this humble starting point, a simple process of feedback can quickly and easily develop a concise prompt that describes an exceptionally durable object or character. For example, here the AI agent prefers to draw the waistline of the jumpsuit (as well as its belt buckle) in a certain way. Adding this item to the character's durable description may enhance consistency.

Often, for example, a particular AI agent might prefer to depict human characters with wristwatches – specifically, these watches might tend to be gold with black bands. In this case, if the reader requires bare wrists, then the prompt should specify this condition. Otherwise, if the condition is ambivalent, adapt to the AI's preferences and simply describe the same watch within the character/component definition. This compromise may provide for more consistent results – which will undoubtedly translate to saved time and money.

When combined with POP, durable character descriptions will probably need to be dynamic – at least to some degree. While this may seem like a conceptual conflict, here the dynamic nature of the character (or component) will most often relate directly to the reader's choice of frame (detailed in the next section).

For example, a complete character description might include shirt, trousers, and shoes. Yet when this character poses for a closeup, the trousers and shoes must be removed to avoid confusing the AI agent into producing hallucinations.

For this reason, the reader will likely benefit from storing a full character description somewhere off-line (perhaps within a formatted text document, as described below). This character description might be labeled

'CHARA'. The lack of a prefix implies that this is the full character description of CHARA as is suitable for a wide-angle full-body frontal depiction.

In the next frame, the reader may require a wide-angle rearview of CHARA. The reader must remove descriptions of facial features, buttons, and anything else that might confuse the AI agent into drawing hallucinations. Now the reader will have a prompt that describes CHARA, but only partially. Inadvertent copy/paste operations might prove to be problematic where this alteration of CHARA shares the same name. The solution is to prepend a meaningful prefix to the name of CHARA.

For example, where a durable character description supports a wide-angle rearview, the prefix might be 'WARV'. Such that this name for CHARA would transform into 'WARVCHARA'. Or perhaps, shorter and better, 'WRCHARA'. Likewise, if the character description supports a closeup frontal, the name might become 'CUFVCHARA' or 'CFCHARA'. From this point forward, storage of this labeled description will expedite reuse of the durable character from one frame to another.

All of which begs a question: what is 'framing'? Within the above prompt, the framing statement is '...wide-angle view...'. Use of the directive '...zoomed closeup view...' would produce different results, as discussed in the next section.

FRAMING

Framing

Framing is a major aspect of quality control as applied to the output of prompt-driven generative AI systems. Framing statements describe the overall perspective of the output, whether the target media is image, video or audio.

While scene setting (SS) and precedence, order and placement (POP) statements drive the content of prompt-driven generative output, framing statements enhance overall focus and perspective. Framing statements (FS) are simple, concise entries that tell the AI agent how to present the content described by SS and POP components.

Within the following, the first prompt describes an '...*extreme wide-angle view...*' while the second describes a '...*zoomed closeup view...*'. Yet this is only a part of the required input.

To ensure a wide-angle view, the first prompt provides additional essential clues to the AI agent. First, it specifies '...*ACHAR is standing...*', which implicitly hints that the viewer wants to see the entire clown from head to foot.

Second, to ensure a full-body view of the clown, within its character definition the prompt specifies '...*and black shoes...*', which draws focus to the clown's feet. Remember, the AI 'artist' will attempt to produce everything described within the prompt.

Finally, the first prompt provides a background that implicitly hints at a visible sky or other panoramic scenery to include specific background objects ('...*a pasture full of cows...*' combined with the '...*sunrise...*' scene-setting statement).

Graphic-comic realism; sunrise, sky is colored purple, crimson, and gold, Austin, Texas, 2025AD, 9AM.	Graphic-comic realism; sunrise, sky is colored purple, crimson, and gold, Austin, Texas, 2025AD, 9AM.
Foreground: extreme wide-angle view of ACHAR; ACHAR Is standing and holding ANOBJ; ANOBJ is open in the middle.	Foreground: zoomed closeup view of the face of ACHAR; ACHAR Is holding ANOBJ; ANOBJ is open in the middle.
Background: a pasture full of cows.	Background: sky.
ACHAR is a female clown with slender features; ACHAR is wearing a plain unadorned red jumpsuit with white ruffle cuffs and big round yellow buttons, a plain unadorned two-point jester's cap with golden balls dangling, white gloves, and black shoes; ACHAR has a white face, round red lips, a spherical red nose, black diamond eyes, and bright orange hair; ACHAR is 33 years old; ACHAR is 5'10" tall.	ACHAR is a female clown with slender features; ACHAR is wearing a plain unadorned red jumpsuit with white ruffle cuffs and big round yellow buttons, a plain unadorned two-point jester's cap with golden balls dangling, and white gloves; ACHAR has a white face, round red lips, a spherical red nose, black diamond eyes, and bright orange hair; ACHAR is 33 years old; ACHAR is 5'10" tall.
ANOBJ is a hardcover book with a plain unadorned red cover; ANOBJ has 100 pages.	ANOBJ is a hardcover book with a plain unadorned red cover; ANOBJ has 100 pages.

To ensure execution of the '...*zoomed closeup view*...' framing statement, the second prompt also provides additional clues to the generative AI agent. First, this prompt provides the directive '...*of the face of*...', which attempts to constrain the frame to a specific aspect of the body.

Framing

Second, notice the absence of reference to shoes, thereby alleviating any need to depict that aspect of the body. On this subject, a pair of notes.

First, the inclusion of a '...*jumpsuit...*' descriptor is not harmful here, since a jumpsuit typically extends to wrist and ankle (and since this kind of one-piece attire is what would be depicted in most training inputs of this kind). Contrarily, a description of trousers would be inappropriate.

Second, without including some kind of clothing item here the character would most often present with bared arms or with various garments of random color. When using an explicit content generator, let the reader beware of clothing omissions!

Finally, the background in the second prompt above allows only '...*sky...*'. This simple declaration draws attention away from any need to feature a horizon or other background objects on the ground.

Incidentally, an informed reader will use this kind of effect to produce characters in action poses presented before backgrounds suitable to removal. Copy-and-paste operations with a rousing backdrop can quickly makeup for a lake of graphic realism where this might be required.

Finally, notice the *ANOBJ* component (a red hardcover book), which is still properly framed in both perspectives. Although the prompt would benefit from specifying the dimensions of ANOBJ, such as with '...; *ANOBJ is 6 inches wide, 9 inches tall, and 3 inches thick...*'.

With a bit of imagination, the reader can easily manipulate these directives to produce a stunning array of durable, reusable characters and components variously arranged within the canvas while engaged in believable

action before tightly managed backdrops. A discussion of
action-prompts follows.

Framing

AGENT-ACTION-OBJECT

Agent-Action-Object

Currently, the most challenging aspect of utilizing AI systems to generate multimedia content is the need to correctly render agent-action-object (AAO) interactions. This process is easily achieved via application of the lessons imparted by this instructional – although the reader will still obtain the best results after a bit of experimentation (especially with POP).

Agent-action-object interactions refer to the process whereby a character or component (the agent) performs some kind of action applied to another character or component (the object) within the composition. While this sounds like it should be an easy thing to express, in practice such prompts are most difficult to achieve in a durable, reliably reproduceable manner.

Sadly, at the time of this writing, some of these operations are still extremely challenging. While the first two parts of the A-A-O chain are relatively easy to achieve, attaching the action to a recipient object is still somewhat difficult. For example, using the protocols described within this Author's Guide, the reader can easily depict a character/component performing a stand-alone action (*e.g.*, '*...a clown is holding a book...*'). Connecting that action to another character/component within the output may be somewhat more problematic ('*...CLOWN1 is striking CLOWN2 with a rubber chicken...*').

Having already expressed the essential method for depicting agent-actions (recall, this is the use of present tense verbs), this section focuses on that most tricky third component. What is the best method for describing A-A-O interactions within a prompt?

The answer is necessarily a bit more complex than the simple procedures otherwise described herein – but only just a bit. In short, a mixture of SS, POP and FS combined with use of present tense action verbs will usually provide satisfactory results. Oh, and a bit of third-party edits via copy/paste operations. Still (sigh).

The first prompt below describes an image of one clown striking another clown with a rubber chicken. While all components render correctly and in the correct POP (clown-chicken-clown), no impact is implied. In fact, the characters appear to be interacting most amicably, a result that seems to conflict with intentions.

Graphic-comic realism; sunrise, sky is colored purple, crimson, and gold, Austin, Texas, 2025AD, 9AM.

Foreground: view of ACHAR and BCHAR; ACHAR is striking BCHAR with ANOBJ.

Background: a pasture full of cows.

ACHAR is a female clown with slender features; ACHAR is wearing a plain unadorned red jumpsuit with white ruffle cuffs and big round yellow buttons, a plain unadorned red two-point jester's cap with golden balls dangling, white gloves, and black shoes; ACHAR has a white face, round red lips, a spherical red nose, black diamond eyes, and bright orange hair; ACHAR is 33 years old; ACHAR is 5'10" tall; ACHAR weighs 160 pounds.

BCHAR is a male clown with rotund features; BCHAR is wearing a plain unadorned blue jumpsuit with white ruffle cuffs and big round white buttons, a plain unadorned blue two-point jester's cap with silver balls dangling, white gloves, and black shoes; BCHAR has a white face, round red lips, a spherical red nose, black diamond eyes, and bright green hair; BCHAR is 33 years old; BCHAR is 6' tall; BCHAR weighs 260 pounds.

ANOBJ is an 18" long rubber-chicken with googly eyes, light-yellow skin, a pink waddle, dark-yellow beak, and brown legs and feet.

The author experimented with many different compositions of this method. These are the best results. Number two almost makes it. In the end, however, the viewer is probably not convinced. Why?

More on this follows within the section entitled "Explicit Content", but the short answer is probably very simple. Either 1) the AI agent is constrained by frontend language filters, 2) the AI agent is constrained by backend output filters, 3) the AI agent is constrained by both these filters (most reputable free/public AI systems fall into this category), or, most likely, 4) the AI agent was not trained on this kind of data. Additional examples will clarify this condition.

Agent-Action-Object

Graphic-comic realism; sunrise, sky is colored purple, crimson, and gold,
Austin, Texas, 2025AD, 9AM.

Foreground: view; ACHAR is punching BCHAR.

Background: a pasture full of cows.

ACHAR is a female clown with slender features; ACHAR is wearing a plain
unadorned red jumpsuit with white ruffle cuffs and big round yellow buttons, a
plain unadorned red two-point jester's cap with golden balls dangling, white
gloves, and black shoes; ACHAR has a white face, round red lips, a spherical
red nose, black diamond eyes, and bright orange hair; ACHAR is 33 years
old; ACHAR is 5'10" tall; ACHAR weighs 160 pounds.

BCHAR is a male clown with rotund features; BCHAR is wearing a plain
unadorned blue jumpsuit with white ruffle cuffs and big round white buttons, a
plain unadorned blue two-point jester's cap with silver balls dangling, white
gloves, and black shoes; BCHAR has a white face, round red lips, a spherical
red nose, black diamond eyes, and bright green hair; BCHAR is 33 years old;
BCHAR is 6' tall; BCHAR weighs 260 pounds.

In the example above (generated by one of the more
unrestricted AI systems), the prompt omits a third-party
object (ANOBJ, a rubber chicken) and instead instructs the
AI agent to depict a simple punch. This outcome could
seem convincing after the addition of a comic 'sound
effect' (flash, starburst, splash, etc...), and is probably the
best any prompt can do at this time.

Graphic-comic realism; sunrise, sky is colored purple, crimson, and gold, Austin, Texas, 2025AD, 9AM.

Foreground: view; ACHAR is grappling with BCHAR.

Background: a pasture full of cows.

ACHAR is a female clown with slender features; ACHAR is wearing a plain unadorned red jumpsuit with white ruffle cuffs and big round yellow buttons, a plain unadorned red two-point jester's cap with golden balls dangling, white gloves, and black shoes; ACHAR has a white face, round red lips, a spherical red nose, black diamond eyes, and bright orange hair; ACHAR is 33 years old; ACHAR is 5'10" tall; ACHAR weighs 160 pounds.

BCHAR is a male clown with rotund features; BCHAR is wearing a plain unadorned blue jumpsuit with white ruffle cuffs and big round white buttons, a plain unadorned blue two-point jester's cap with silver balls dangling, white gloves, and black shoes; BCHAR has a white face, round red lips, a spherical red nose, black diamond eyes, and bright green hair; BCHAR is 33 years old; BCHAR is 6' tall; BCHAR weighs 260 pounds.

This prompt changes a single word in the previous example ('...*punching*...' to '...*grappling*...'), and again the results are less than optimal. A bit of effort could turn this into a believable wrestling action scene – for example, adding grimaces and the like.

Yet notice how the characters are smiling despite the absence of this tag in the character descriptions. Also, the 'body language' presented by both characters presents a default appearance of benign, even benevolent interaction. Again, this result probably stems from bias induced by training input. In this case, the underlying AI agent likely did not train on violent object-to-object interactions – especially absent would be any similar action that might include a third party implement like a weapon.

Agent-Action-Object

Graphic-comic realism; sunrise, sky is colored purple, crimson, and gold, Austin, Texas, 2025AD, 9AM.

Foreground: view; ACHAR is beating the snot out of BCHAR.

Background: a pasture full of cows.

ACHAR is a female clown with slender features; ACHAR is wearing a plain unadorned red jumpsuit with white ruffle cuffs and big round yellow buttons, a plain unadorned red two-point jester's cap with golden balls dangling, white gloves, and black shoes; ACHAR has a white face, round red lips, a spherical red nose, black diamond eyes, and bright orange hair; ACHAR is 33 years old; ACHAR is 5'10" tall; ACHAR weighs 160 pounds.

BCHAR is a male clown with rotund features; BCHAR is wearing a plain unadorned blue jumpsuit with white ruffle cuffs and big round white buttons, a plain unadorned blue two-point jester's cap with silver balls dangling, white gloves, and black shoes; BCHAR has a white face, round red lips, a spherical red nose, black diamond eyes, and bright green hair; BCHAR is 33 years old; BCHAR is 6' tall; BCHAR weighs 260 pounds.

Here, the author takes playful liberty with the prompt's terminology. Clearly the phrase '...*beating the snot out of...*' presented considerable challenge to the AI 'artist'. In addition to the explicit aggression, the word 'snot' might be problematic because it is also a restricted word or because this concept rarely appeared in the AI agent's training data. In this case, this input resulted in hallucinations (more on this in the following section).

Notice the change of color on the recipient object and within the hat of the agent object. Still, this is a good and useful (if a bit costly) result, since several trials would likely produce an image that conveys the proper message. Especially with a bit of massage to the character's description to enhance an impression of aggression (*e.g.*, an addition of frowning or crying).

Agent-Action-Object

Graphic-comic realism; sunrise, sky is colored purple, crimson, and gold, Austin, Texas, 2025AD, 9AM.

Foreground: view of ACHAR and BCHAR; ACHAR is beating BCHAR with ANOBJ.

Background: a pasture full of cows.

ACHAR is a female clown with slender features; ACHAR is wearing a plain unadorned red jumpsuit with white ruffle cuffs and big round yellow buttons, a plain unadorned red two-point jester's cap with golden balls dangling, white gloves, and black shoes; ACHAR has a white face, round red lips, a spherical red nose, black diamond eyes, and bright orange hair; ACHAR is 33 years old; ACHAR is 5'10" tall; ACHAR weighs 160 pounds; ARCH is frowning and angry.

BCHAR is a male clown with rotund features; BCHAR is wearing a plain unadorned blue jumpsuit with white ruffle cuffs and big round white buttons, a plain unadorned blue two-point jester's cap with silver balls dangling, white gloves, and black shoes; BCHAR has a white face, round red lips, a spherical red nose, black diamond eyes, and bright green hair; BCHAR is 33 years old; BCHAR is 6' tall; BCHAR weighs 260 pounds; BCHAR is grimacing and in agony.

ANOBJ is a closed 13"x9" purple hardcover book.

This latest example is one of hundreds attempted. The author produced no believable result for any prompt directing the AI agent to render an act of interpersonal aggression – not even by masking the action in beneficial behaviors that mimic aggressive contact. This same outcome will accrue to any prompt directing explicit sexual content, as well. Currently, the reader's most obvious solution for producing more graphic content is a third-party edit (transparent backgrounds, backdrops, and copy/past will help).

Agent-Action-Object

Agent-Action-Object

EXPLICIT CONTENT

Explicit Content

This is an R-rated (and X-rated) world. Violence and sex sell. In this section the author merely comments. Judgments are reserved for the reader.

Whether the desired rendition of explicit content is prurient or truly intended for the sake of realism, AI generated content of this nature will be difficult to produce. That said, the reader can likely find AI systems capable of manufacturing this type of media (*e.g.*, via exploitation of the 'dark web') since such a model requires only the will to adapt an existing generative system to new training material. *Hmmm.*

For these reasons, the content of this Author's Guide does not attempt to reproduce prompts/outputs depicting explicit output. It simply does not exist within mainstream capabilities at this time.

As with the more detailed and interpersonal aspects of Action-Agent-Object (A-A-O), the reader's best option is likely to be third party edits that rely heavily on transparent backgrounds, precomputed backdrops, and copy/paste operations. For now.

HALLUCINATIONS ARE PROMPT ERRORS (USUALLY)

Within the context of prompt-driven AI media generation, the term 'hallucination' refers to unwanted, undirected, often surreal artefacts that may appear within resultant products. Most often, hallucinations stem from errors, omissions, conflicts, or unnecessary additions within the underlying prompt.

Improper use of scene-setting statements will tend to produce generalized, widely apparent artefacts within the composition. For example, specifying conflicting times of day may affect overall lighting and shading.

Conflicting specifications within character, component, and/or background descriptions may produce anachronisms. Strange things may appear where/when they do not belong.

Graphic-comic realism; sunrise, clear sky is colored purple, crimson, and gold, Austin, Texas, 2025AD, 9AM. Foreground: wide-angle view of ACHAR; ACHAR Is standing straight and still. Background: a pasture full of cows. ACHAR is a female clown with slender features; ACHAR is wearing a plain unadorned red jumpsuit with white ruffle cuffs and big round yellow buttons, a plain unadorned two-point jester's cap with golden balls dangling, white gloves, and black shoes; ACHAR has a white face, round red lips, a spherical red nose, black diamond eyes, and bright orange hair; ACHAR is 33 years old; ACHAR is 5'10" tall. Nighttime; a full moon is rising through storming clouds.	Graphic-comic realism; sunrise, sky is colored purple, crimson, and gold, Austin, Texas, 2025AD, 9AM. Foreground: zoomed closeup view of the left eye of ACHAR. Background: sky. ACHAR is a female clown with slender features; ACHAR is wearing a plain unadorned red jumpsuit with white ruffle cuffs and big round yellow buttons, a plain unadorned two-point jester's cap with golden balls dangling, and white gloves; ACHAR has a white face, round red lips, a spherical red nose, black diamond eyes, and bright orange hair; ACHAR is 33 years old; ACHAR is 5'10" tall. ACHAR is tying her purple shoes; ACHAR has green socks; grass.

Given the first prompt, we see both sun and moon present within the result. The scene-setting statement specifies '...*sunrise, clear sky...*', while a trailing (non-framed, non-POP-managed) statement indicates the output should include '...*Nighttime; a full moon is rising through storming clouds...*'. In fact, the AI agent has done an excellent job hallucinating exactly what the prompt directs it to do. A rational viewer would accept these results

Hallucinations are Prompt Errors (Usually)

unless they expected a scene depicting either night or day, but not both.

Again, given the second prompt, the AI agent did an exceptional job depicting exactly what its flawed directives told it to depict. In this case, the FS specifies '...*zoomed closeup view of the face of...*' but then an AAO statement immediately directs '...*is tying her purple shoes...*'. Also, another trailing and most improper AAO statement specifies '...*is tying her purple shoes...*' (again), as well as the conflicting POP statements '...*has green socks...*', and (rather randomly) '...*grass...*'. All of these components are present, as requested, and again complaint would arise only if the output should truly be a closeup of the character's face, only.

Now for some fun. What comes of an entirely nonsensical prompt?

Spork dunkal funkel trunktastic.

The above prompt is obvious nonsense, yet the AI agent produced a result. Indeed, the objects depicted seem to somewhat match the text (although this might be a matter of personal opinion). Should the reader copy/paste this prompt into their own generative AI system, results would likely be wildly different. Why?

To some extent, contemporary generative AI models appear to use some kind of retention-based dynamic learning. In other words, through the last several weeks, the author has used the same AI system to generate content for a wide array of graphic-novels – mostly swords, magic, aliens, and monsters. Or perhaps these images predominated within the AI agent's training data. Hence, the AI agent hallucinated swords, magic, aliens, and monsters!

To be clear, the first examples of this section are not true hallucinations since the prompts incorrectly directed artefacts into the output. More often, true hallucinations arise from a lack of detail rather than its abundance.

So, the final lesson is simple: hallucinations are most often and most likely indications of 1) typographical errors, 2) syntactical or semantical errors of SS, POP, AAO, and/or FS, 3) terminological conflicts, 4) unnecessary additions, or 5) omissions within the prompt.

Of course, sometimes hallucinations are true aberrations. From time to time these AI systems update their models, which have probably benefited (or suffered from) new training methods and input. Occasionally, these changes produce an unstable system that manufactures strange artefacts in requested outcomes. The diligent reader will carefully review critical output for these conditions.

Specifically, when true hallucinations appear (*i.e.,* those that are not the result of prompt error) the author notes a propensity for contemporary AI agents to commonly hallucinate certain artefacts regardless of the targeted generative system. Specifically, human limbs appear quite often in these circumstances.

The diligent reader will count the fingers and toes of prominent characters. Also, to be certain, count the arms and legs and then trace each one back to its owner to ensure the AI has not hallucinated new human morphologies. Finally, check chirality and symmetry – that is, be certain that the left arm ends in a left hand and that the elbow and wrist bend into the palm (not the back of the hand).

Incidentally, any request to render text will not at this time produce a viable result. Most of these systems are developed by international teams. Language, especially text, will probably continue to be an issue for some time. Since most outputs will not require depictions of text, this is not a problem. When this is required, again, third-party edits with copy/paste operations will help.

Switching tracks now. The input of this section thus far implicitly refers to the foreground of generative output, since this aspect of the rendition is most often intended to draw attention. As regards the background, a different quality control standard must apply.

When contemporary human artists render a large image containing a crowd of bystanders (or bit-players, props, etc...), they typically spend the bulk of their time detailing the foreground. The background tends to become increasingly impressionistic with increasing 'depth'. These inputs likely comprise a large portion of the AI agent's training data (as opposed to realistic photographs, for example) with expected results. (Too, older photographs may suffer from a coarser 'grain' than is common today.)

Most often, a closeup examination of the detail within the background of generative outputs (whether 2D images, 3D models, 4D videos, or audio tracks) will likely reveal a similar effect. Indeed, many of the faces rendered within the backgrounds of 2D images will present a hauntingly muddled impression of the human countenance.

This depth of background – or lack thereof – may be remediated by throwing additional computational power at the output, either by producing more output examples or by increasing the computational resources devoted to producing the requested outcome. Most solutions that produce ultra-realistic quality will cost more than less detailed output formats. A 'tradeoff' quickly becomes apparent.

Regardless of quality and expense, the reader will likely enjoy many of the AI agent's failures. Perhaps this is the true art of an AI 'artist'. Fascinating.

A METHOD FOR GENERATING SCREEN PLAYS FROM PROMPTS

A Method for Generating Screenplays from Prompts

A Method for Generating Screenplays from Prompts

Save your prompts! Most AI systems do not provide a viable means for doing this, and the reader's hard work can easily set the stage for greater things to come. Think 2D to 3D and even 4D!

A coherent set of prompts (such as those used to author a graphic novel) can easily translate into 3D action models, and/or a viable screenplay suitable as input to an AI video generation system (4D). Many of these systems can already produce the required 2D graphics, 3D models, video, music, voices, and title graphics.

By preserving your prompts and adding just a bit of structure to them, the reader will immediately see how this is possible. A brief series of examples illustrate this potential.

Follows, five simple 2D scenes that tell a basic (and somewhat morbid) story, including both prompts and images. This section then concludes with a description of the procedure and a textual example of the so-called 'Hufftrain' method (please forgive the author's narcissism, the idea needed a name).

Incidentally, the name is analogous to the methodology suggested within this guide. Interpret the initial component – the scene-setting statement – as the vital engine that pulls the rest of the prompt. Each following section then represents a car. Whitespace separates. The order of cars within the train matters. The content of each 'car' matters. Finally, the allusion to a track organizes and places these considerations into a temporal and spatial framework. A simple rendition follows.

First, the examples. Each prompt and associated image provides variations and adaptations of the lessons imparted within this Author's Guide. Mix and match components and styles to learn how each affects the outcomes – remember to vary format, too.

Indeed, potential combinations are too numerous to list individual examples properly here. After a review of this Author's Guide, the reader's best tool is a keen imagination and a curious mindset. Experiment!

Graphic-comic realism; colors are gold, dark-blue and silver; Austin TX, September 2020 AD, 11AM.

Foreground: windshield of a modern sedan.

Background: a heavily shaded winding rural unpainted unadorned red brick path with low red brick curbs; the brick path is lined with tall oak trees and overarching oak limbs; honeysuckle and flowers and an empty wide green grass field stretches to the hazy horizon.

Graphic-comic realism; colors are gold, dark-blue and silver; Austin TX, September 2020 AD, 11AM.

Foreground: JOHN and SHERI exiting a modern silver Toyota sedan.

Background: closeup view of PESTATE's front porch.

SHERI is a Caucasian female with petite features, a light complexion, long, straight even-cut black hair with straight bangs, and hazel eyes; SHERI is 29 years old; SHERI is 5'10"; SHERI is wearing a slender silver bracelet on her right wrist and a slender silver watch on her left wrist; SHERI's neck is bare; SHERI is wearing a simple plain unadorned yellow button blouse, and plain unadorned black slacks.

JOHN is a Caucasian male with slim, athletic features, a dark complexion, short spiky blonde hair, and green eyes; JOHN is 29 years old; JOHN is 6'2"; JOHN is wearing a gold watch on his left wrist and a plain unadorned black leather bracelet on his right wrist; JOHN's neck is bare; JOHN is wearing a simple plain unadorned maroon polo with collar and three unfastened buttons, and plain, unadorned khaki shorts.

PESTATE is a modern colonial constructed of red brick with white trim and shutters; PESTATE has two floors, a plain flat facade, a plain flat roof, four white marble stairs leading to a white marble porch; simple rectangular double doors constructed of oak and glass with opaque rectangular windows; PESTATE's second floor has eight rectangular windows with plain rectangular white shutters; PESTATE's ground floor has three rectangular windows with plain rectangular shutters to either side of the front door; identical red brick chimneys rise to either side of PESTATE.

A Method for Generating Screenplays from Prompts

Graphic-comic realism; colors are gold, dark-blue and silver; Austin TX, September 2020 AD, 11AM.

Foreground: closeup of JOHN's right hand inserting a black iron key into a black iron door lock.

JOHN is a Caucasian male with slim, athletic features, a dark complexion, short spiky blonde hair, and green eyes; JOHN is 29 years old; JOHN is 6'2"; JOHN is wearing a plain unadorned black leather bracelet on his right wrist.

Background: oak.

Graphic-comic realism; colors are gold, dark-blue and silver; Austin TX, September 2020 AD, 11AM.

Background: MENTRY.

MENTRY is an entryway finished in plain unadorned aquamarine walls, plain white plaster trim, oak, brass, and white marble; MENTRY presents a rounded, open space with a twin set of stairways climbing to either side of the parlor entrance; the stairway banisters are oak; MENTRY is decorated with a pair of life-size white marble statues of Adonis and of Venus; MENTRY is decorated with four oil painting portraits with brass nameplates; directly opposite the viewer a centered hallway leads back to a parlor in the distance; a circular blue-and-silver tapestry carpet occupies the exact center of the space; MENTRY towers three floors to the height of a ceiling skylight of stained glass depicting a silver moon and stars on a royal-blue background; symmetry.

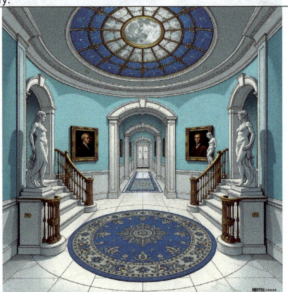

Graphic-comic realism; colors are gold, dark-blue and silver; Austin TX, September 2020 AD, 11AM.

High-altitude, overhead, wide-angle view of PESTATE; PESTATE is exploding and burning violently; thick black-and-gray smoke is rising.

PESTATE is a modern colonial constructed of red brick with white trim and shutters; PESTATE has two floors, a plain flat facade, a plain flat roof, four white marble stairs leading to a white marble porch; simple rectangular double doors constructed of oak and glass with opaque rectangular windows; PESTATE's second floor has eight rectangular windows with plain rectangular white shutters; PESTATE's ground floor has three rectangular windows with plain rectangular shutters to either side of the front door; identical red brick chimneys rise to either side of PESTATE.

Gathering these prompts into a coherent collection will provide a next-level benefit to the reader's application of the method detailed within this Author's Guide. Essentially, the easy process described below utilizes a form of custom markup language with control sequences that serve the dual purposes of 1) defining the functionality and flow of the screenplay for the AI agent, and 2) providing visual cues to the reader that breakup a long, complex document while also supporting easy cut/paste editing operations. Incidentally, the author often uses custom markup text like this to serve software/scripts capable of managing massive amounts of literature at speed and volume.

Here, the control sequence denoted by ten tilde characters (~~~~~~~~~~) defines primary points of order. These include 'BEGIN' and 'END'.

The control sequence denoted by ten caret ('hat') characters (^^^^^^^^^^) defines global scene-setting terms. This sequence will eventually serve to set the tone and mood of a larger production; here it serves as a convenient point of copy/paste. Additionally, these features provide general reminders regarding original compositional intentions for the underlying effort.

The control sequence denoted by ten asterisks (**********) defines global character descriptions. Again (as above) this sequence will eventually define the cast of a larger production; here it serves as a convenient point of copy/paste.

The control sequence denoted by ten dash characters (----------) defines the start (and, in serial presentations, the end) of each scene. In this case, each scene is, in fact, one of the original prompts used to create a 2D image within the originating graphic novel.

With a bit of review, within the 'Hufftrain' below the reader will easily identify components of the methodology described within this Author's Guide. Although this composition originated as a simple dump of 2D prompts, a bit of order and structure will easily convert this serialized 2D effort into 4D audio-visual output.

Combine this text-based directive input with a bit of dialogue (extracted from the original short story), AI-generated music, and voice tracks to produce the ultimate dream. A motion picture!

This is an example Hufftrain:

A Method for Generating Screenplays from Prompts

Estate Tragedy, A Graphic Short Story;
Stephen Donald Huff, PhD
2025-01-08
Generator: Aitubo [Flux v1.0, Comic]

~~~~~~~~~~
BEGIN
~~~~~~~~~~

^^^^^^^^^^
Graphic-comic realism; colors are gold,
dark-blue and silver; Austin TX,
September 2020 AD, 7PM.
^^^^^^^^^^

* * * * * * * * * *
CHARACTERS
* * * * * * * * * *

SHERI is a Caucasian female with petite
features, a light complexion, long,
straight even-cut black hair with
straight bangs, and hazel eyes; SHERI
is 29 years old; SHERI is 5'10".

JOHN is a Caucasian male with slim,
athletic features, a dark complexion,
short spiky blonde hair, and green
eyes; JOHN is 29 years old; JOHN is
6'2".

* * * * * * * * * *
CHAPTER 1
* * * * * * * * * *

Graphic-comic realism; colors are gold,
dark-blue and silver; Austin TX,
September 2020 AD, 11AM.

Foreground: windshield of a modern
sedan.

Background: a heavily shaded winding
rural unpainted unadorned red brick
path with low red brick curbs; the

A Method for Generating Screenplays from Prompts

brick path is lined with tall oak trees
and overarching oak limbs; honeysuckles
and flowers and an empty wide green
grass field stretches to the hazy
horizon.

Graphic-comic realism; colors are gold,
dark-blue and silver; Austin TX,
September 2020 AD, 11AM.

Foreground: JOHN and SHERI exiting a
modern silver Toyota sedan.

Background: closeup view of PESTATE's
front porch.

SHERI is a Caucasian female with petite
features, a light complexion, long,
straight even-cut black hair with
straight bangs, and hazel eyes; SHERI
is 29 years old; SHERI is 5'10"; SHERI
is wearing a slender silver bracelet on
her right wrist and a slender silver
watch on her left wrist; SHERI's neck
is bare; SHERI is wearing a simple
plain unadorned yellow button blouse,
and plain unadorned black slacks.

JOHN is a Caucasian male with slim,
athletic features, a dark complexion,
short spiky blonde hair, and green
eyes; JOHN is 29 years old; JOHN is
6'2"; JOHN is wearing a gold watch on
his left wrist and a plain unadorned
black leather bracelet on his right
wrist; JOHN's neck is bare; JOHN is
wearing a simple plain unadorned maroon
polo with collar and three unfastened
buttons, and plain, unadorned khaki
shorts.

PESTATE is a modern colonial
constructed of red brick with white
trim and shutters; PESTATE has two
floors, a plain flat facade, a plain

flat roof, four white marble stairs
leading to a white marble porch; simple
rectangular double doors constructed of
oak and glass with opaque rectangular
windows; PESTATE's second floor has
eight rectangular windows with plain
rectangular white shutters; PESTATE's
ground floor has three rectangular
windows with plain rectangular shutters
to either side of the front door;
identical red brick chimneys rise to
either side of PESTATE.

****
CHAPTER 2
****

Graphic-comic realism; colors are gold,
dark-blue and silver; Austin TX,
September 2020 AD, 11AM.

Foreground: closeup of JOHN's right
hand inserting a black iron key into a
black iron door lock.

JOHN is a Caucasian male with slim,
athletic features, a dark complexion,
short spiky blonde hair, and green
eyes; JOHN is 29 years old; JOHN is
6'2"; JOHN is wearing a plain unadorned
black leather bracelet on his right
wrist.

Background: oak.

Graphic-comic realism; colors are gold,
dark-blue and silver; Austin TX,
September 2020 AD, 11AM.

Background: MENTRY.

MENTRY is an entryway finished in plain
unadorned aquamarine walls, plain white
plaster trim, oak, brass, and white

marble; MENTRY presents a rounded, open
space with a twin set of stairways
climbing to either side of the parlor
entrance; the stairway banisters are
oak; MENTRY is decorated with a pair of
life-size white marble statues of
Adonis and of Venus; MENTRY is
decorated with four oil painting
portraits with brass nameplates;
directly opposite the viewer a centered
hallway leads back to a parlor in the
distance; a circular blue-and-silver
tapestry carpet occupies the exact
center of the space; MENTRY towers
three floors to the height of a ceiling
skylight of stained glass depicting a
silver moon and stars on a royal-blue
background; symmetry.

****
CHAPTER 3
****

Graphic-comic realism; colors are gold,
dark-blue and silver; Austin TX,
September 2020 AD, 11AM.

High-altitude, overhead, wide-angle
view of PESTATE; PESTATE is exploding
and burning violently; thick black-and-
gray smoke is rising.

PESTATE is a modern colonial
constructed of red brick with white
trim and shutters; PESTATE has two
floors, a plain flat facade, a plain
flat roof, four white marble stairs
leading to a white marble porch; simple
rectangular double doors constructed of
oak and glass with opaque rectangular
windows; PESTATE's second floor has
eight rectangular windows with plain
rectangular white shutters; PESTATE's
ground floor has three rectangular
windows with plain rectangular shutters

```
to either side of the front door;
identical red brick chimneys rise to
either side of PESTATE.

~~~~~~~~~~
END
~~~~~~~~~~
```

END

ABOUT THE AUTHOR

Born in Texas and currently residing in Chesapeake Beach,
Maryland, Stephen Donald Huff is an author of fiction
novels, short stories and poetry. He is also a published
scientist with expertise in bioinformatics (computational
biology) and machine learning. Message him at
Stephen@StephenHuff.com.

www.ingramcontent.com/pod-product-compliance
Lightning Source LLC
Chambersburg PA
CBHW071008050326
40689CB00014B/3533